T0195016

Why MS Has Destroyed My Life

Why MS Has Destroyed My Life

Dr. Jill Silver, MS, DDS

WHY MS HAS DESTROYED MY LIFE

iUniverse books may be ordered through booksellers or by contacting:

iUniverse
1663 Liberty Drive
Bloomington, IN 47403
www.iuniverse.com
844-349-9409

Because of the dynamic nature of the Internet, any web addresses or links contained in this book may have changed since publication and may no longer be valid. The views expressed in this work are solely those of the author and do not necessarily reflect the views of the publisher, and the publisher hereby disclaims any responsibility for them.

Any people depicted in stock imagery provided by Getty Images are models, and such images are being used for illustrative purposes only. Certain stock imagery © Getty Images.

ISBN: 978-1-6632-3942-6 (sc)
ISBN: 978-1-6632-3941-9 (e)

Library of Congress Control Number: 2022909553

Print information available on the last page.

iUniverse rev. date: 08/02/2022

The interpersonal effects of having a chronic disease: multiple sclerosis

It's about MS and is about how this disease altered my entire family.

It started on a Tuesday, and it has influenced and changed my life forever. My forearm became numb. Not pins and needles numb, just dead to the touch, and it was obvious something was wrong. I was a junior in dental school and although I felt despair, I

completed school, graduating on time. I was ready to face the world. It started so gradually and innocuously that it almost seemed untrue as I went for an MRI and waited to hear the outcome. I was told that my case would not amount to anything, so I trusted the doctors who proudly gave me their diagnosis over the phone at Columbia University. It all unfolded, and I vowed to keep it a secret, adopting the approach that it was no one's business as no one could offer me any solutions. Since MS did not have a cure then and still doesn't, I lived with this sad truth for years,

living symptom-free and loving my life. I went on to have two beautiful children and settled down to work in a dental practice. It never plagued me early on, so I truly forgot about it.

So, my life began, and I took it by storm, enjoying every minute with very few bumps in the road.

One significant occurrence was the development of endometriosis, which happened after the birth of my first child, which clearly indicated that I was autoimmune. Another contributing piece of evidence that supported the fact that I suffered with widespread

autoimmunity was my anaphylactic reaction to pignoli nuts, which has persevered throughout my life, and I always must fear the dreaded evil pine nut and anything in pesto sauce. I also have severe reactions to metals that aren't pure and suffer horribly with contact dermatitis, which is also autoimmune in nature.

Life unfolded for me in glorious ways. I got married to a fabulous man and we moved from Long Beach to Merrick when our older child was in first grade and tried our best to enter an unfriendly

and competitive community. I was working so my MS went unnoticed.

My first real exacerbation was during the summer months, and it hit me like a ton of bricks and brought me to my knees with very confusing symptoms.

I could not stay awake and when I did my head was all wrong. I had feelings of always being dizzy and I found myself struggling to see. I had trouble with my gait and stride and also constantly felt what only can be described as altered sensations throughout my body. I relied on a heavy dose of steroids to propel

me forward and made an appointment with my very first neurologist. After waiting hours to see him, he walked in the office to hit my knee with a replica of a hammer and then started pushing a medication on me that did not disclose how it acted to help me and it also had a garden variety of scary side effects. We were travelers back then and had made a wonderful trip to Cabo, so I sat at the infinity pool and took the new medication every day and continued to take it for a year. My very first MRI showed that after a year consuming this med and losing a good part of my hair

and raising my blood pressure through the roof that it was actually doing more harm than good, and I had to cease taking it. I continued seeing Dr. H Until one of his assistants called me spastic and that ended my relationship with him even though I thought he had a certain magic about him with his love for Monaco and his adoring term of "bubella." How can I be insulted and mistreated for something that was clearly not my fault? I then took the approach of alternative medicine and laid low for a few years, relying on my good sense and optimism and did not

darken the door of another neurologist until I came across one who not only suffered with this disease himself but actually shared my alma mater. Cornell has always been a strong thread through my entire life. I married the son of a true icon that was on faculty there and my love for the school deepened. This neurologist seemed like the perfect fit and although he believed in traditional medicine, I still was still on a path to pursue alternatives and stem cell therapy.

Things were going OK in my corner of the world or so I thought but while I

was consumed with keeping this secret of sorts, things started to unravel in a way I never anticipated. My pillar, my love, started to feel underappreciated and started to look outside our marriage to deceive me and sadly broke my heart and our vows to be forever loyal to one another and had a brief affair. I was devastated and felt betrayed and powerless because he chose to do with her the one thing I could not do much of, which was to walk. Who taught him to be a man, one who could support a sick wife and not stray from our marriage, I'll never understand. I had so many

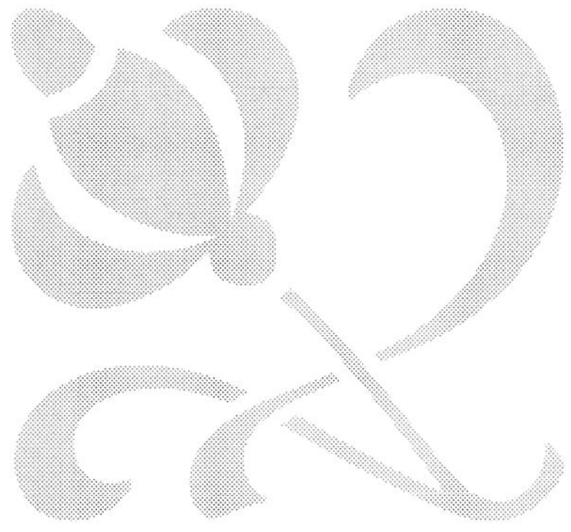

questions and although he was there for me in every way, he was not in my court resenting me for his doting behavior because he had completely snapped and acted out of character and did the unthinkable. I never denied him sex so this was uncalled for and very deceitful. He was right. I was aggravated with this awful disease and hurtful and at times extremely discourteous, but that is not a valid reason to betray someone. Whether it was a mid-life thing or propagated by my illness, it happened and could only be sorted out in therapy. My man, who I was counting on for

life hurt me deeply to my core but my need for his love never wavered. I was disgusted that he let another into our bedroom and exposed me to germs and diseases I thought I would never be exposed to because we promised each other our love for life. He felt underappreciated and taken for granted and oh so lonely all the time, having to go places on his own, but I was battling a serious disease all on my own and it had consumed me. How could I ever forgive his transgression while I was protecting us both from the perils of COVID, using sterilizer in each load of

laundry while he is lying in bed with another woman who was unhappy in her own marriage. What a huge slap in my face, and all I can do is continue my twenty-five-year marriage to a man I loved and try to mend our alliance for my own sake, for life without him would prove to be lonely and hard. You see, we had become a machine of caretaker and recipient. He was everything to me in every way, so it became a no-choice option. If I was going to persevere, I had to keep him in my life and learn to forgive him. That did not come easy for me because I adored him and the

thought of loaning him out to sleep with another made me instantly want to vomit and throw him out once and for all. What was going on in his head that he threw his righteousness out the window, I guess I'll never know. The trust was gone forever. Every time he left our home, my mind went to that place where he deceived me and met with this woman and things had not changed at all here at home because he was still home by 5 and preparing dinner. How can I ever trust his word again because he behaved like a frat boy on spring break but I can't live

like that so I forced myself to believe him and accompany him where I could and be the kind of wife he needed and deserved. It was hell because, at fifty-six, who needs this, and I could never let him go because I still loved him and admired all he was doing for me. It was very hard because I was forever paranoid that he was taking another lover because, sadly, my man openly lied to me. On top of it all I never feared this with him because he was a man of values and ethics that ran deep. I could not ever do that to him because I am not built like that, and I was previously

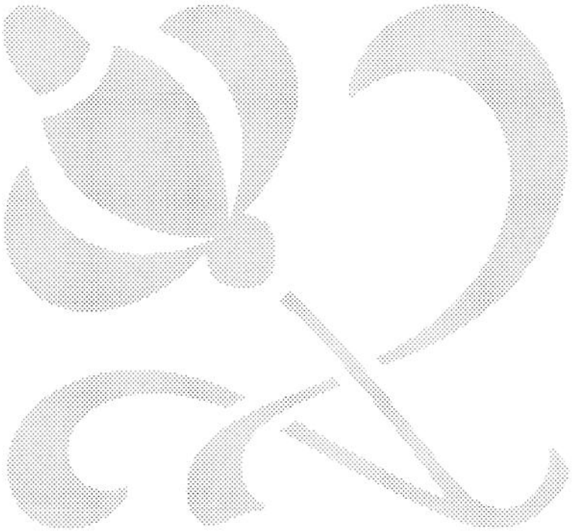

sure neither was he, but I was dead wrong. He crossed a very serious line which involved our vows and G-d and my definition of marriage.

MS had now taken my life and my marriage and all my dignity, so I was reeling with sadness and anger, and I had nowhere to turn. It had destroyed everything in its midst. What a truly awful disease and although I was up for the fight, sadly my husband was not. He had filed for divorce and was not letting it go. He was still pursuing things with the attorneys, and I felt pressured, and I felt that things were the same

as always. We shared what I thought was a fairy tale of existence, peppered with joy and the usual disagreements and I could not understand his desire to end things after such a long and beautiful marriage. We had traveled the world even with my scooter in tow and I trudged along lovingly as much as I could and believing our marriage was stronger than ever.

We have two adult children who are both magnificent and engaging. My daughter has never understood or honored my ailment like I have believed she should. Sadly, it stands as a deterrent not a

unifier. I love her always, but I cannot understand her lack of humility at all. Sure, she is well adjusted and likable in all ways. She has almost taken a stance that somehow, I am milking my ailment and she continues to only be supportive of her father. I was always an excellent mother to her for as long as I could be, not being able to walk or drive, but sadly, MS robbed me of a relationship with my only daughter. She's engaged now to a fabulous young man, and he is perfect for her but also perfect for us as a family. I can't help but want a closer relationship with her, and I wish she

understood the absolute hell that I live with day in and day out, but I really never included her in my full diagnosis because I never wanted her to worry about me or be consumed with it at all, so it was easier to deny it and lie about it. I told my son on a college trip to the University of Rhode Island and just my mere mention has made him aware and highly considerate. He always offers his help to me, which I often refuse out of some invisible pride. I am hoping my daughter can be an avid part of my life in time. Mending things with her is paramount to me and I would love

to return to the days that MS had not fully altered all our lives, but sadly it will need some work on everyone's part to get there.

My new drug is a true blessing in every way. I spent my entire life avoiding taking medication for my MS because of my immobilizing fear of the side effects that they all carry, and I felt protective of the excellent health I had, except for MS. Why would I open a door to potential cancer or blood disorders when I enjoyed my otherwise incredible health? For years, I was plagued with horrendous knees, crying each time I sat

on a too-low toilet for fear I would never be able to get up. I would dread entering a public bathroom, anticipating that the handicapped accessible bathrooms were always in the rear of the bathroom, making my trip quite difficult crossing the entire length of the room. My fear extended to making my life easier by wearing adult diapers so I could easily be prepared for release while I was out of the house. We learn, we improvise to minimize embarrassment. It's survival at its most basic core and it's something I do not share with the masses. This new drug (vulmerity) is a game changer.

It seems to check all the boxes, being in pill form and not being an injectable or infusion because I dread anything relating to needles, being terribly vasovagal. Perhaps it is helpful that I am finally being treated for a disease that I suffer with or perhaps it is the anti-inflammatory component that benefits my knees, but suddenly I'm not plagued with my usual joint issues. I'll take that as a win-win.

All in all, this has been a bear for me. I had to give up a career as a dentist, which I trained for, devoting so much time and money on. I have lost all

self-respect and I have lost my one true love but with patience and care perhaps I can come out a winner and hopefully enjoy good times ahead. I certainly hope and pray to. This is my story and it's akin to most of us who suffer in silence as the bearer of an invisible ailment. I have MS, but it doesn't have me.

Printed in the United States
by Baker & Taylor Publisher Services